Art of Insomnia

poems

by

Peter A 28.04.22

D1637501

First published 2021 by The Hedgehog Poetry Press

Published in the UK by
The Hedgehog Poetry Press
5, Coppack House
Churchill Avenue
Clevedon
BS21 6QW

www.hedgehogpress.co.uk

ISBN: 978-1-913499-35-8

For Helen

forever

Contents

I   BEAUTIFUL / TERRIBLE

BEAUTIFUL/TERRIBLE

You gave us

the most beautiful Easter

Sun shining like no other Easter

Most terrible terrible Easter

Most beautiful woman

Most terrible

terrible

loss

YOUR FACE IN OILS

Your face in oils
I fail to render,
each new day lives
in memory

Your grace in tears
washed bright by terror,
your caring eyes
forever see

Until our souls
return together,
your beauty will
still visit me

HELENIUM ONE AND ONLY (*Helenium sui generis*)

Environmentally friendly but with low disease immunity,
of the Helianthus hybrid, a threatened rare variety.
Compared to the usual sunflower surprisingly small,
so unassuming you would not associate the two at all.

Blossoms with maturity, from being a wallflower
to leaving lasting impressions upon all who see her.

Never disappointing while growing and blooming
but, when without warning there occurs an uprooting,
be aware that her removal leaves a gaping hole -
a space hard to fill in any way meaningful.

II   FRENCH RETREAT

NEARLY NOT GOING OUT SYNDROME

Call it a syndrome if you wish.
If you're anything like me
it'll happen when you agree
that you'll attend a soirée
or even a daytime affair
but when the time comes
you're not quite sure
if you really want to be there.

Sometimes you give yourself a wee shove
and get ready, maybe arrive just on time.
Other times the effort is just too much
and you abandon the battle without really trying.
It isn't laziness - it's just your head isn't right

The most extreme example experienced by me
of the paralysing effect of this mentality
was the painting holiday.
Three months after such a loss,
a few hours before my flight
and in the dead middle of night
I stared at the un-ironed unpacked clothes
wondering if I should get on with preparation
or just abandon the whole vacation.

It could have gone one way or the other;
I had reached the stage of thinking it didn't matter.

I think I did the right thing getting my head together
to go.

If I had given in and stayed at home
that would have been the right thing too.

You don't know until you do whatever
you eventually choose to do.

PILGRIMAGE

just three months after
and too soon to travel
- some must have thought

from those who love me
surely too distant
- the South of France

but I have to escape
the persistence of kindness
- mix with strangers instead

to meet a challenge that
could not be taken lightly
- less time for overthinking

and it is tough
using oils for the first time
- a steep learning curve, in my case a mess

least talented there
attempting portrait in landscape
- hung out to dry in the sun

just what my soul needs
sharing air creatively
- dining in their revelry nightly under stars

a chance to be me
with those who do not know me
- do not know the silence I take back to my room

only one day off
from hard work and company
- the day I carry your light in my heart to Lourdes

FOUND IN FRANCE

Though you would have to concede
its picture perfect rural beauty
here for the record are the things
you wouldn't like about the place.

The middle of the countryside
such a distance from anywhere.
The crowded transport
transferring from the airport.
The open windows to keep the place cool
inviting houseflies.
The doorway dogs, the ever-darting
omnipresent lizards.
The lack of television .
The steps, useful for others,
which would be impossible for you.
Around those steps the lavender
which at home would aid your sleeping
but here for you a nightmare,
attracting wasps and bees.
The spider's improbably small body,
impossibly spindly long legs,
waiting in the shower room, patiently.
Also the tiny white spider
- I bet you never saw an entirely white spider!
The mosquitoes, the hornets.
The blood-sucking horseflies
almost certainly lining up to feast upon
you in particular.
The bats awaiting
the chance to be entangled in
your lush long hair.
The swimming pool that would be out of bounds for you.
The conversation in which you would not wish to speak.

The revelation before bedtime
concerning the cleaner's cat,
its trophy mice and
the minor flea infestation
- *successfully eradicated we think*
but let us know if you get bitten.

As for me,
the only aspect of the French place
I do not appreciate
is you
not being here.

III RETURN TO WHAT REMAINS

ANNIHILATED

Will I
be reduced to
nothing?

Am I a fool
to think
I can survive
my heart's
cold removal,
the loss
of what kept me
alive?

BETTER FAIL

Some people think you're better
than you actually are
and if you try to tell them otherwise
they just won't accept it.
They will brook no protest, no confessional
and your soul shrinks from absence of forgiveness.
So you tell yourself you're going to be better
than you actually are
just to re-balance the scale.

Some people think you're braver
than you actually are
and if you try to tell them otherwise
they just won't accept it.
They will brook no protest, no sign of weakness
and your heart is strained from absence of empathy.
So you determine you're going to be braver
than you actually are
knowing you're destined to fail.

ACTING THOUGH

Though dramatic tears
may have been expected
the waiting audience
was left disappointed.

Though in moments still
quiet teardrops spill
not the cataracts
which mark out other acts.

Though in private scream
and often ask just why
I strut my time on
stage barely moist of eye.

Thus do I act strong
when I lack all kinds of strength;
Thus do I make sense
when nothing at all makes sense.

Yes, I know.

Acting though.

A KIND OF ACCEPTANCE

More than six months on
waking up this morning
for the first time instantly knowing
that which on every previous waking
took seconds to sink in.

The everyday reality of
just one person's tragedy
which in this case I embrace as mine.
Unimportant to the wider world.
Minuscule in the grand scheme.

But there it is clear at last
even in my brain's first yawn.
The hope of miracles
or release from that recurring nightmare
finally completely gone.

SURVIVAL GUILT

Now in mornings waking,
no one to be kissed,
spend some time convincing
myself I still exist.
Why do I go on living
if to help no one?
What point is there existing
now that you are gone?
Knowing it's a blessing
still to be alive;
yet it is distressing
you are not by my side.
Your tender touch is missing,
your eyes of sapphire blue.
Your heart so full of feeling
and loyalty so true.
That is why this morning
though I can see and breathe,
I take some time considering
what I do and don't believe.

A HOUSE IS NOT A HOME

A house is not a home.

Only people make homes
though a house,
as a pet does,
may develop characteristics
of its owner.

This house still holds
your voice and more.

ATTRACTIVE PART

Content am I to walk through life
invisible, obscure

She always was the better, the
attractive part of me

That people loved her, reflected
some glory on me too

Her dependence on me gave me
a status undeserved

A better man for having known her,
lesser now that she is gone

A weight gone you think, burden lifted -
this lightweight now heart-heavy

CHRISTMAS CARD TO HALF A PERSON

Today I received the first card
of this Christmas Season.
Today I received a greeting
addressed to half a person,
the lesser half
that is not you.

More cards I know will come
and it may seem to some
ungrateful that I do not
send them greetings in return.
But I cannot.
My right hand gone.

AFTER THE ENDING

As I started
to avoid some of those
who knew the situation
and loneliness became
an attractive destination
I found myself
befriending
not the sort of friends
that we together would have made
but the sort of friends
who come with the new role that I played,
a role which held little interest
for the friends we already knew

I do not chase friends
in an active way
but wait for them to come to me.
I care not if I don't agree
with every aspect of their lives.
If in them a good person I see,
If they have a spirit that's calling to me,
If they have talent and ability,
that's all to be encouraged
A world of art and love and spirituality
is my antidote for the world's poison
I need this energy to elevate me
during the public hours
before I go home alone and quiet to be.

Discovering others brave
as you were brave,
Appreciating courage more
because I witnessed yours.
Those I meet don't know the reason
for my wide-eyed admiration.
I leave it parked well out of sight
to remain a secret to all except the very closest
or sometimes those I know I won't meet again.
A gift offered quietly just before parting

IV INSOMNIA

CUT ADRIFT

It started as cowardice
Afraid of going to bed
Afraid of going to sleep
Afraid of not waking up

Although I missed your voice I was
Afraid of hearing from you
Afraid of what you thought
A child afraid of ghosts

Though those fears have gone
The seemingly illogical hours
The turning night into day
all reflects my life capsized

I now accept and understand
this is not a passing phase
Whatever days remain for me
I shall spend them tossed by waves

A SHOCK TO THE SYSTEM

It isn't deliberate,
this going to bed as daylight returns.
It isn't something I have set out to do.
I am not afraid
to sleep in the dark.
The blinds and the curtains
and sometimes the bedclothes
combine to give morning a semblance of night
as I retire.

I doubt if I can give
an explanation which satisfies logic
so I won't try, save to say that I think
I have had what my old mum would
describe as a shock to the system.
It feels like my life has lost all its rhythm.
When the heart beat returns, if it returns,
what remains of my life will probably be alright
and then expire.

ACCIDENTAL SUNRISE POETRY

this time it's a post on Facebook
the image a tripod with camera
the photographer's words confirming
he has just set up to capture
dramatic shots of sunrise
and I haven't gone to bed yet
wasting time on social media but
I've written a poem by accident

A LITTLE NIGHT MUSIC

Of course there are the sounds of nature,
The other night was torrential rain,
Every morning the dawn chorus.
The sounds that were always there for us
even if we did not notice
when tv and radio and chatter filled the brain.

But in the silence of your passing
there comes previously unheard noise.
The minor and normally ignored sounds,
The creaks of movement in our house,
The whirring of the shower room fan,
All convert to music and voice to fill the void.

BACKGROUND NOISES

Everything sounds different
in the dark
The crumple of a plastic bag
given life
Drips of water, the paw-steps of
small creatures
I can almost hear you giggling
in the night

A PLAN FOR INCREASED EFFICIENCY

(Theoretical, awaiting further scientific investigation before experimentation on living creatures, a description which no longer applies to me)

No longer am I deluded
having tonight concluded
that I no longer want to sleep
Though dreams are desired by me
the time wasted with eyes closed
could certainly be better used
if I did not succumb to slumber
plugged instead into a battery charger
so that I may carry on dreaming
yet continue work unsleeping
Unceasing carry on unsleeping
Unceasing carry on unceasing
Unceasing carry on unsleeping
Unceasing carry on

NINE MINUTE INTERVALS

Nine minutes
since snooze was pressed

Alarm rings
and is snoozed again

It's an act
of volition but is it voluntary?

A habit
formed of laziness

Or a sign
of reluctance to face the world?

What do you
during nine minute intervals?

Do you rest
or practise breathing?

Prepare for the battle?

ACKNOWLEDGEMENTS

Two men named Mark are due my grateful thanks:

I am indebted to Mark Davidson of Hedgehog Press. Had he not selected these poems for publication, they would have remained inside my heart and laptop but would not be available in their current form; and

Mark Mutch O'Hare for flattering portrait photography as well as his essential contribution to cover artwork.

Thereafter, I have to thank three women who have been integral to the whole process:

Firstly, Gaynor Kane for insightful close reading of earlier drafts of *Art of Insomnia*, and invaluable suggestions which led to important improvements;

Secondly, Anna Saunders for confidence-building encouragement and support, as well as her close reading and valued endorsement of the final draft of *Art of Insomnia*; and

Finally, Helen who is at the centre of this writing and to whom I owe eternal gratitude.

Peter A
December 2020